The Christ Mind

The Great Source of Unlimited Power

By William S. Hyatt, D.D.

The Christ Mind

The Great Source of Unlimited Power

By William S. Hyatt, D.D.

PYRAMID PRESS

Copyright © 1982 USESS

All rights reserved. No part of this book, in part or in whole, may be reproduced, transmitted, or utilized, in any form or by any means, electronic or mechanical, including photocopying, recording, or by any information storage and retrieval system, without permission in writing from the publisher, except for brief quotations in critical articles, books and reviews.

International Standard Book Number-10: 0-9899017-8-5
International Standard Book Number-13: 978-0-9899017-8-9

First Pyramid Press Edition 2016

The paper used in this publication meets the minimum requirements of the American National Standard for Permanence of Paper for Printed Library Materials Z39.48-1984

PYRAMID PRESS
9550 South Eastern Avenue • Suite 253
Las Vegas, NV 89123 U.S.A.
contact@pyramidpress.net

Dedicated to
The CHRIST MIND in
EVERY MAN/WOMAN.
May all become AWARE of HIM,
and follow HIS path.

We are pleased to present the Christ Mind Power Series. We hope you receive as much understanding and inspiration as we have in its preparation.

The postscript to this book contains pertinent information about the philosophy and doctrine of the Church of the Guardians and a partial list of services which we offer.

May you find the abundance, joy and success which HE has set aside for you.

The use of the terms "man" and "he" throughout this book is a gender-neutral pro-noun, referring to any person in general, such as person, mankind or humans. The capitalized version of "Him" refers to Christ.

Introduction

Many people often ask the questions, "What is the purpose of life? Why do so many of us suffer?" Life for many seems filled with obstacles and pain, so much so that many people surrender to unhappiness and failure. People harm and take advantage of each other so much that it often seems that evil outweighs good.

But, in spite of this despair, there lies a hope in each and every person for a better and more meaningful life. Sometimes we remember God and His Son in the recesses of our mind, but often this trickle of hope is drowned out by our day to day struggles in life.

Some people go to church and on that day appear to believe in Him and His *promises*, but a few minutes after the service is over, revert back to despair, forgetting all about God and his love.

Men and women truly want a better life for themselves and others, but their deep rooted insecurities and fears drive them to do things which they know at their core, are harmful and wrong.

We of the Church of the Guardians believe that the answer to people's despair and insecurity lie within themselves. We believe that the *spark* of God lies within each person, dormant and unused. People have forgotten the promises of God, hence they have fallen into despair. When men and women remember their *true identity*, and through proper teaching and techniques, learn how to connect with their *divine nature*, they will free themselves from frustration, despair, loneliness and insecurity. We believe that the *dormant seed* of the Christ Mind is in all people; and that its *immense power* is available to help them in this life so that they may *join* more with Him now and in the future.

To this end the Church of the Guardians have dedicated this book to help in the awakening and utilization of the Christ Mind so that people can live more successfully in the service of His purpose.

We hope this book will help those who are desirous of awakening their *true identity* so that they may help others who wish to do the same.

We are also available for guidance, education and prayer and we hope that you seek our help in your quest for self-development. To this end we offer this prayer:

> *May you find the abundance, joy and peace which*
> *He has set aside for you.* —*Amen.*

Sincerely, The Church of the Guardians

Table of Contents

Introduction		vii
Chapter 1	The Christ Mind, The Great Source of Unlimited Power	1
Chapter 2	The Christ Mind and Successful Living	13
Chapter 3	Theory and Methods of Adoration	31
Appendix I	The Goals of the Church of the Guardians	41
Appendix II	Activities and Services	45
Appendix III		47
	The Philosophy	
	The Precepts	
	The Essence	
Appendix IV	The Academic Programs	63
Selected Book List		97

Chapter 1

The Christ Mind
The Great Source of Unlimited Power

"If thou would'st hear the Nameless, and wilt dive into the Temple-cave of thine own self, there, brooding by the central altar, thou may'st haply learn the Nameless hath a voice, by which thou wilt abide, if thou be wise."

—Tennyson

The Christ Mind is God's *greatest gift* to humankind. The Christ Mind is that part of each person which is the essence of Christ. It contains unlimited power, love, and creative force. Every person has the Christ Mind within but few are aware of its presence or know how to utilize its greatness.

"Though man is one with the *higher power* which may be called God, the fact remains that he has lost the consciousness of this unity. And unless he makes the effort, as in regular meditations, frequent self-observation, or in true prayer, to detach himself from his external existence it is unlikely that he will recover this *divine consciousness*."

—Paul Brunton

The essence of the Christ Mind can be gleaned from these words. Each person has within him a *divine friend* whom he doesn't know. The Christ Mind lives deeply in every person, but few know how to reach it. The person who sacrifices his falseness and works towards the Christ Mind will obtain perfection and union with God from whom the *power* of everything comes. Those who seek and find this *divine friend* within will see the truth of His wisdom, and be *one* with Him.

"He who is concerned about his life shall lose it; and he who loses his life for my sake shall find it."
Matthew 10:39

St. Augustine expressed his feeling in this way. *"I, Lord, went wandering like a strayed sheep, seeing thee with anxious reasoning without whilst thou wast within me.... I went around the streets and squares of the city of this world seeking thee; and I found thee not, because in vain I sought without for him, who was within myself."*

When inquiries are made as to the methods of contacting the Christ Mind, it must be remembered that contact is not made by willpower alone working through the conscious mind. The Christ Mind is quiescent to the conscious mind and requires illumination by God. Even though the Christ Mind cannot be reached through willpower alone, there are a number of techniques available which can be used to become receptive to the Christ Mind.

"We cannot kindle when we will the fire which in the heart resides; the Spirit bloweth and is still. In mystery the soul abides."
—Matthew Arnold

TECHNIQUES FOR THE DEVELOPMENT AND USE OF THE CHRIST MIND

1. Determination: This is best expressed as firmness of *purpose*. If a person wants and believes in a better life he must resolve himself to this end. He must realize that this can only be accomplished through the awareness and utilization of the Christ Mind.

2. Belief: To accept as true that God's *great gift* to mankind is the Christ Mind, which contains unlimited power, love, and creative force.

3. All removal of all negativism, cynicism, stubbornness, ego centeredness, preconceived ideas, and infantilism: The personal ego is eliminated from the center of awareness and replaced by the Christ Mind.

4. Work: Effort and dedication are necessary to discover and utilize the Christ Mind.

5. Concentration: Often people believe that whatever appears in the mind is purposeful, meaningful, and reflective of their true self. Concentration differs from normal thinking in that it is intentional and focused. Concentration allows the choice of *purposeful* and *powerful* thoughts, rather than weak and meandering associations. True concentration transforms a mind weakened by past circumstances into a mind that lives harmoniously in the present and has power over the future.

6. Prayer: Prayer is not rote repetition of phrases, but instead a directed form of living energy aimed at a specific request from God.

7. Meditation: The mind engages in continuous and directed contemplation on meaningful thoughts and symbols. This process clears the mind from extraneous chatter, allowing the Christ Mind to emerge.

8. Adoration: This is an emotion of profound admiration, love, and devotion. The emotion is attached to the virtues of the image or idea and attempts are made to integrate the qualities into the personality.

9. Will: Will is the deliberate choice of ends and actions. The *discovery* of the Christ Mind is quickened through **deliberate acts** which serve the *will* of God, i.e., giving, loving, helping, and healing.

10. Affirmation: This is the process of saying *yes* to *life* by opening consciousness to the Christ Mind.

11. Questioning: The process of the mind which uncovers preconceived ideas and beliefs which block the path to the Christ Mind. In addition, character traits of selfishness, stubbornness, and ego centeredness must be uncovered and removed. For some people this can be a painful process.

MANKIND'S PURPOSE IN THIS WORLD

God made humans to serve as His representative on Earth and into human's hands *He* placed the *trust* of the world.

Man must not be blinded by his body, mind, instincts, nor his ego. We call these four the *lure*. Man's attraction to the *lure* must be tempered. The richness and vastness of his *life* is lost when the Christ Mind is hidden under the *lure*. This attraction and preoccupation is understandable, although undesirable. The *lure* was created for man's use and joy. However, he must not surrender his entire being to the *lure*, but instead, place it in proper perspective. When men place the Christ Mind in the center of consciousness, war, pain, and disharmony will end and man will win his true prize, **immortality**. As long as man is attracted solely to the *lure*, rather than being Christ Mind-centered, immortality would be the greatest danger to mankind and the world. As God said in Genesis 3:22, *"The man has become like one of us, knowing good and evil; what if he now reaches out his hand and take fruit from the tree of life also, eats it and lives forever?"*

Each person's purpose is the mastery of self and the world. This is accomplished through self-development, serving others, *creation*, *love*, and following the contextual meaning of God's laws.

This is clearly expressed in Ecclesiasticus 17:1-14, from the Apocrypha. The Lord created man from the earth and sent him back to it again. He set a fixed span of life for men and granted them authority over everything on earth. He clothed them with strength like his own, forming them in his own image. He put the fear of man into all creatures and gave him lordship over beasts and birds. The Lord gave them the use of the five faculties; as a sixth gift he distributed to them mind, and as a seventh, reason, the interpreter of those faculties. He gave men tongue and eyes and ears, the power of choice and a mind for thinking. He filled them with discernment and showed them good and evil. He kept watch over their hearts, to display to them the majesty of his works. They shall praise his holy name, proclaiming the grandeur of his works. He gave them knowledge as well and endowed them with the life-giving law. He established a perpetual covenant with them and revealed to them his decrees. Their eyes saw his glorious majesty, and their ears heard the glory of his voice. He said to them, "Guard against all wrongdoing", and taught each man his duty towards his neighbour.

POWER

To accomplish his purpose in the world, each person must have **power**. Power is the force that moves the world. The *greatest power* available to humans comes from the Christ Mind.

> **"Man, ignorant of self, creates his own unhappiness. The world masters him, when he was born to master the world. Life comes down with cruel feet, sooner or later, upon every man who knows few or many things but does not know himself."**
> **—Paul Brunton**

THE POWER PRINCIPLE

Power under purpose is the **power principle**. This is the development of **power**, through the awakening of the Christ Mind within, to serve the *purpose* of *creation*, *love* and *self mastery*.

Power without *purpose* is *emptiness*, and *purpose* without *power* is *nothingness*. Both *power* and *purpose* are essential for successful living.

GOD'S WORLD OF ABUNDANCE

When the Christ Mind is in control of a person's life and he has use of its powers, he begins to experience and enjoy the abundance of God's love. He becomes a master of circumstances and perceives reality clearly. This makes him a powerful instrument in God's blueprint of life.

> **"The spirit must enter into every department of a man's life: If he leaves it out of his business activities, if he forgets it when dealing with other people, he shuts himself out of its magical power to give him the truest success, the greatest happiness, and the most harmonious existence."**
> **—Paul Brunton**

WE ARE ALL LIVING BUT ARE WE ALIVE?

All that breathe are living but only those who have opened themselves to the Christ Mind are alive. The Christ Mind is the vital link to a vibrant purposeful life.

> "The lamp of your body is your eye; when therefore our eye is bright, your whole body will be lighted; but if it is diseased, your whole body will also be dark."
>
> **Luke 11:34**

MAN IN TROUBLE

Man's troubles disappear when he develops a living awareness of the Christ Mind, and knows how to utilize its unlimited *power* to serve the *purpose* of man and God.

> "Because I had forsaken unity with thee, because I, fool had made my body me, because I did not know thee who didst dwell in me, therefore I wandered through raging hells...because I threw away my very self, I therefore was in chains."
>
> —Unknown

MAN'S/WOMAN'S ACT OF CREATION

> "I have said, You are gods; all of you are children of the Most High."
>
> **Psalms 82:6**

An ultimate *act* of man is creation. Through this process he/she brings into existence useful, pleasurable, and meaningful experiences and accomplishments. The act and process of creation permeates the world with the energy of *love*, which heals the wounds of the world.

HEALING THE SELF AND THE WORLD THROUGH THE ACTS OF CREATION

Man heals himself, others, and finds *purpose* through acts of creation. Success in this area requires knowledge of the creative cycle which allows man to overcome obstacles. Complete understanding of this cycle helps man from being discouraged and blinded by depression, frustration, hostility, jealousy, and feelings of helplessness.

THE CREATIVE CYCLE

The *creative cycle* has four parts.

1. The Spark: This is the desire and enthusiasm which initiates creation. From this a great outpouring of energy is experienced. This energy gives vitality and instills a sense of *power* and *love*.

2. The Disappointment: Often there follows displeasure with the initial spark. A feeling of disappointment and disillusionment arise as internal obstacles appear to block the creative urge. Frequently, the spark is extinguished. Instead of becoming discouraged, man must learn to change inner obstacles into challenges. He re-lights the spark by overcoming the challenges with the aid of the Christ Mind.

3. Frustration and Anger: External obstacles begin to interfere with the spark. Feelings of anger and frustration appear overwhelming. Man must change these external obstacles into challenges and overcome them with the help of the Christ Mind.

4. Victory: The goal is perfected and achieved. A great joy of completeness is felt and the capacity for living is increased. Man feels totally free and *one* with God and fills the world with love and happiness.

MAN'S ACT OF KINDNESS AND JUSTICE

Learning to treat himself and others with kindness and justice heals the wounds of the world.

MAN'S ACT OF UNION

Man accomplishes *union* with God through the **awakening** and use of the Christ Mind. This ecstatic state is an experience which allows man to proceed to higher levels of objective clarity.

> **"Be still, and know that I am God."**
> **Psalms 46:10**

THE TRUE LOVE OF OTHERS

True love of others occurs when there is a joining of *two* or more Christ Minds. Other forms of *love* are personal, meaningful and necessary, but they are not the same as the *union* of *two* or more Christ Minds. The *true love* experience is spontaneous and cannot be willed.

MAN'S OBLIGATION

Man's duty and obligation is to experience the joys and abundance of life by *creation, love*, and the *administration* of God's *trust*. Man is loved and cherished by his *creator*.

The Father demands that his law be obeyed and that man finds his way to Him, through the Christ Mind.

> **"For this commandment which I command thee this day, it is not hidden from thee, neither is it far off. It is not in Heaven, that thou shouldest say, who shall go up for us to Heaven, and bring it to us, that we may hear it, and do it? Neither is it beyond the sea, that though shouldest say, who shall go over the sea for us, and bring it unto us, that we may very nigh unto thee, in thy mouth, and in thy heart, that thou mayest do it."**
> **Deuteronomy 30:11-14**

TO THIS END WE PRAY

Let us visualize a planet where human beings are guided by the Christ Mind. Imagine millions of humans setting into motion immeasurable quantities of *love, joy* and *energy.*

Life will be successful in a world governed by the power and love of the Christ Mind.

TO THIS END WE SERVE

Chapter 2

The Christ Mind and Successful Living

The person who truly lives the successful life understands himself and experiences the Christ Mind that God has provided. He has an awareness of his *inner essence* and complete faith in his uniqueness. He manifests great vitality. He does not live in fantasy, but instead, lives within the stream of action in the world. He rides the wave of natural harmony within himself and rejoices in the light of his victories.

This successful person recognizes that the **purpose** of his earthly existence is the mastery of himself and this world through *creation* and *love*. Having this goal in mind, he diligently works towards that end. His accomplishments on earth provide him with a feeling of joy and completeness.

A person of **purpose** leads a life filled with power, richness, and joy. He avoids boastfulness and arrogance. He is deeply involved with his Christ Mind and realizes the potential for the actualization of *man's purpose* in the world.

MAN'S JOY

Following the path of *creation* and *love* is the crux of the *divine purpose*. Man's obligation to God is to create a successful and joyous life. Man becomes guilty when he shuns his obligation to perfect God's *purpose*—man's mastery of himself and this world through deeds of *creation*, *love*, and the utilization of God's greatest *gift*, the Christ Mind.

SHARING GOD'S GIFTS

Knowing that God expects him to fulfill his purpose in the world, the successful person shares his gifts with those around him. He realizes that man is the best loved of all God's creations and acknowledges this fact by improving himself and helping others.

THE OBLIGATION TO CREATE A SUCCESSFUL LIFE

Many people feel that they cannot create a successful life. However, the fact is that they can. Creation is achieved through effort, belief, knowledge, and action. Working at successful living is the first step in satisfying man's obligation. God has provided all the necessary tools to accomplish this end. When man fulfills his obligation, he is rewarded with the feeling of *joy*.

MEN AND WOMEN BELONG TO GOD

Man belongs to the Lord and is special to Him. This makes him ultimately unique, the property of no one, including the state, relatives, friends, or one's mate. Man is a possession of the Lord and no other person or group has a claim to his life. Life belongs to man and man belongs to God, no more and no less.

TO THIS END WE PRAY

I AM
THE PROPERTY
OF THE LORD

I HAVE THE RIGHT TO MY LIFE,
AND ULTIMATELY
THE POWER TO BRING FORTH
LOVE
HEALTH
HAPPINESS
SUCCESS
WEALTH
I AM A GUARDIAN OF HIS TRUST.

HAPPINESS

All men pursue *happiness* in one form or another. In fact, man has the God given right and duty to pursue happiness.

Happiness is but an experience and a momentary sensation. It is not something that can be touched or held in one's hand. Happiness is something which occurs; it cannot be owned. It is fleeting, ephemeral and enjoyable. It is the result of *creating, loving*, doing, accomplishing, and living according to His *purpose*.

Happiness occurs whenever man improves his physical or spiritual condition. This has been man's responsibility for thousands of years. Man must constantly seek means of improving himself, and creating happiness in the world. Man's desire of well-being, pleasure, and giving love and joy to others must be at the heart of all he undertakes. When man has successfully accomplished a worthy task, he must enjoy his accomplishment. From this he finds replenishment and his body and joy for his spirit.

HAPPINESS AND SUCCESS

Happiness and success are closely related, happiness often being the direct result of success. Although success is not the same for everyone, it is something that everyone seeks. Success ranges from specific accomplishments such as getting a job, finishing a project, accumulating wealth; to generalities like being successful or leading a contented life. Man must remember that success is both general and specific. Goal related success occurs when there is success at a specific goal. It is important to see the difference between the idea of general success and specific success. If a person is a success at his job and a failure in his marriage, is he then a success or a failure? The answer is simply that he is a success at his job and a failure at his marriage. **We are only a complete success (the general) when our lives are governed by the Christ Mind and we fulfill God's purpose of creation.**

NON-INTERFERENCE POLICY

Man, in his pursuit of happiness and successful living, has no right to forcibly interfere with another's pursuit of the same goal. Man is a unique and unprecedented entity. His desires, no matter how similar to those of others, are specifically his and his alone.

All men serve God's purpose in different ways and at different times. Few men can honestly say they have the understanding, wisdom, and insight to evaluate and label another's progress or purpose, and even fewer men would want their goals and actions interpreted and judged by another.

> **Once you label me,**
> **you negate me.**
> **—Kierkegaard**

A rule for successful living is that no one forcibly interfere with another person's pursuits or goals. It is not man's duty nor obligation to approve of, or disapprove of another's way of life, unless he has been rightfully assigned the role of judge. All people have the right to choose where and how they live, as long as they do not violate another person's property, or the *principles* and *laws* of God.

Matthew 7:12 expresses this in the following manner: Judge not that you not be judged. For with the same judgement that you judge, you will be judged, and with the same measure with which you measure, it will be measured to you.

POSITIVE SELF-IMAGE

A positive self-image is an important and necessary aspect for successful living. A man who doesn't like himself and treats himself poorly is a poor representative of God's intentions. If man is to enjoy life and develop his power (Christ Mind) and fulfill God's purpose, it is essential that he cultivates this capacity for self-worth.

Feeling good about oneself is a state of mind, an attitude, something which develops through the accumulation of positive experiences. A positive self-image, like the rays of the sun, radiates to others, increasing their joy and capacity for living. It starts with a smile and a kind word. These things spread positive affirmation and doesn't cost anything. Some find it's actually easier to be nice than to be mean.

LAW OF ATTRACTION AND RETURN

A wise person discerns what he thinks, says, and does, for he realizes that the "Law of Attraction" is a fact of life. Guaranteed failure and self-negativity in word and deed— words, images, and deeds cast upon the waters of life shall return as cast. This is called the "Law of Eternal Return". Every thought, deed and word returns to you sooner or later with astounding reliability.

LAW OF DECLARATION

The power of the spoken word and thought is immense. Man can attract either positive or negative experience and things through his words and thoughts. Whatever is voiced and held in the mind will sooner or later come to pass.

> **Death and life are in the power
> of the tongue.**
> **—Proverbs 18:21**

> **A sorrowful person grieves himself; from
> his own mouth comes his destruction.**
> **—Proverbs 16:26**

> **He who slanders in heart will not find good; and
> he who has an evil tongue falls into mischief.**
> **—Proverbs 18:20**

> **A man's belly shall be satisfied with the
> fruits of his mouth; and with the fruits
> of his lips shall he be filled.**
> **—Proverbs 18:21**

WORK IS THE ESSENCE

When the power of the Christ Mind is contacted through the various techniques outlined, (see pages 3-4) life will be filled with happiness and success. God requires that man actively do his share as a necessary condition for success. As God worked so must man.

> **But Jesus said to them, My Father works
> even until now, So I also work.**
> **—John 5:17**

THE COURAGE TO BE

Successful living requires that man have the *courage to be*. This means the *courage* to *live* as he *thinks* and *knows*. *True courage* is manifested or shown by the *action* a person takes when he is in trouble, and when he is successful. A person who seeks God only in times of difficulties, misuses the *ideal* of God, and doesn't understand His way. Similarly a person who forgets God when things are going well and prides himself alone on his good fortune is not only vain, but weak.

When a person has *courage* to be a *child* of God, and acknowledge the *true power* within him, he finds *grace* in the eyes of the Lord. Belief in God must be manifested at every opportunity. God is always there; *He* awaits your awareness of *His* presence. This is beautifully expressed by the poem "*Footprints*".

> **One night a man had a dream. He dreamed he was walking along the beach with the LORD. Across the sky flashed scenes from his life. For each scene, he noticed two sets of footprints in the sand; one belonged to him, and the other to the LORD.**
>
> **When the last scene of his life flashed before him, he looked back at the footprints in the sand. He noticed that many times along the path of his life there was only one set of footprints. He also noticed that it happened at the very lowest and saddest times in his life.**
>
> **This really bothered him and he questioned the LORD about it. "LORD, you said that once I decided to follow you, you'd walk with me all the way. But I have noticed that during the most troublesome times in my life, there is only one set of footprints. I don't understand why when I needed you most you would leave me."**
>
> **The LORD replied, "My precious, precious child, I love you and I would never leave you. During the times of trial and suffering, when you see only one set of footprints, it was then that I carried you."**
>
> —Author Unknown

INNER CHANGES — OUTER CONSEQUENCES

The only change that can ever bring about a lasting and satisfying change of affairs occurs internally. Man's life circumstances depend on accepting this truth. If conditions are to be changed, first work must be applied within. Occurrences in the outside world are a reflection of the inner world. Looking outside for a change or solution often leads to failure and disappointment, unless we first make a commitment to change and then follow through.

BODILY HEALTH

Exercise and maintenance of the body is necessary to insure its proper function. It is foolish to allow the body to decay through abuse and lack of activity. The body should be given at least an hour of exercise every day. The diet should be satisfying and balanced. Occasional indulgence is necessary to satisfy the body's cravings. By consciously giving in power is gained over its cravings thereby reducing the energy necessary for self control. We believe that the best way to control the body's excessive demands is to recognize them and give in to them willfully. Excessive control of the body are "exercises" of the will, and not virtues as some believe.

ILLNESS

Illness is often a signal that something is wrong in the way of life. The cause of illness or disease can stem equally from germs and attitudes. When a person is ill his whole life-style must be examined. Examination of the body alone is insufficient for a total cure. Spiritual, mental, social, interpersonal, and dietary factors must be explored fully. In modern language this is called holistic medicine, although this approach has been used since the beginning of civilization.

THE CURE OF ILLNESS

A cure can arise from various forms of treatment, be they medical, psychological, spiritual, or otherwise. However for any particular method to find success, three ingredients are required.

a) The patient's willingness and desire to get well.
b) The operator's (physician, faith healer, etc.,) belief and knowledge of his craft.
c) God's Power.

When all three factors are present the result is improvement.

WEALTH

The belief that the accumulation of wealth is not a desirable goal has come from the misinterpretation of God's *purpose*—the mastery of this world and this life. Possessing wealth or seeking wealth is a very important aspect of successful living. The danger of wealth stems from those who believe that monetary wealth can substitute for spiritual wealth. The misconception that everything would be "great" with the possession of wealth is very naive and limits the vastness of the human experience.

> **...My sons, how hard it is for those**
> **who trust in their wealth to enter**
> **into the Kingdom of God!**
> **—Mark 10:24**

Wealth is a manifestation of God's power on earth, and reflects "God's Law of Abundance". God's power is infinite, He is the ultimate supplier. Man must learn to accept all that God has to offer. Wealth is also a great responsibility and a man who misuses this gift shall be judged harshly. Wealth must be used to expand man's service to the Lord through helping others and rejoicing in the Lord's *abundance*.

Wealth is created by accepting the challenge of life. The mind must remain open to new opportunities, and the creative process must be allowed to flow. All energy directed towards negativity and failure must be removed. Gather useful information at every opportunity and perform the necessary techniques religiously.

One final point on wealth, when you achieve it, never forget that it is a gift from God who placed it in your hands for *trust*.

> **For worldly people seek after all these things; and your Father knows that these things are also necessary for you. But seek the Kingdom of God, and all these things shall be added to you.**
> **—Luke 12:30-31**

> **And he said to them, take heed what you hear; with what measure it will be measured to you again and will increase, especially to them who hear. For to him who has will be given; and from him who has not, even that which he has will be taken away**
> **—Mark 4:24-25**

SUCCESSFUL RELATIONSHIPS

Man requires the companionship of his fellow beings, yet often finds himself/herself disappointed and angered in this pursuit. Sometimes the cause of hurt and anger arises from lack of specific knowledge concerning human interaction. While a complete discussion of interpersonal relationships is beyond the scope of this book, we will provide an outline and guide which will be helpful in improving relationships.

THINGS TO REMEMBER IN STRIVING FOR GOOD RELATIONSHIPS WITH FRIENDS AND FAMILY

Individual Differences: An apple is an apple and an orange is an orange. As simple as this may sound, when applied to human relationships, it is difficult for many people to refrain from trying to make another person over. *People should be accepted as they really are and enjoyed or avoided on that basis*. Great joy and pleasure are provided by relationships when they are selected for their essence and potential.

Learn to Ask Directly: Do not hesitate to ask for what is wanted or needed. True strength and love is shown when a person can admit to his needs and desires. Some people are more aware of their needs than others. Each person must evaluate and determine what his/her true needs are and seek them religiously; never forgetting that no person or persons can substitute for the Lord or the ultimate *power* of the Christ Mind.

Appropriate Involvement: Do not become inappropriately involved with people or situations. Be cautious of those who are demanding and do not respect your uniqueness. Be careful of those who demand immediate intimacy, usually this person is overwhelmed by his own needs and fears and will sooner or later devour your time or dislike you intensely. Always attempt to surround yourself with people who provide joy, knowledge, and comfort.

Be Reasonable: Unsuccessful relationships develop when unreasonable demands are made on yourself and others. All anyone can do is their best. Being content with this, will lead to relaxation and happiness—and inevitably the ability to do better later.

The Demand for Perfection: Perfection is an ideal toward which to aim, but it's achievement is futile, since the ideal itself changes each time a new plateau of development is reached.

> **Jesus said to him, "Why do you call me good? There is no one who is good except the one God."**
> **—Mark 10:18**

Man must learn to accept himself as he is at each moment. He must refuse to permit others to make unreasonable demands on him and if they persist, ignore them. Put a quick stop to unreasonable demands. Once a person has made up his mind that he will no longer tolerate unreasonable demands for perfection (whether from himself or someone else) often the demands will stop automatically.

Fear of Loosing Love: Never fear loosing someone's love through being your *true self*. If their love is lost for this reason, it was not worth having in the first place. Shakespeare put it well: *TO THINE OWN SELF BE TRUE, and thou canst not then be false to any man.*

PARENTS AND CHILDREN

Parents can't choose their children and children can't choose their parents. While both may want to like each other this is sometimes difficult. It is impossible to be all things to all people all the time.

As a child becomes an adult, it is difficult for both parent and child to realize the need for a change in relationship. The son or daughter must now take on the responsibility of depending on themselves, seeking support from the parent only in emergencies. Parents must continually realize that their "role" as protectors and guides has been diminished and their service along these lines is often more harmful than helpful. Maintaining the parental "role" far beyond its time leads to neurotic dependency for both parties.

It is non-productive, disappointing and impossible to hold on to the past. Carl Bard says it this way:

> **Though no one can go back**
> **and make a brand new start,**
> **my friend,**
> **Anyone can start from now**
> **and make a brand new end.**

Another expression of this principle can be found in this verse by the Guardians.

> **Parents bless your children**
> **and let them be.**
> **Give them what you can**
> **and set them free.**

RELATIVES

Tension associated with relatives is caused by the refusal to *consciously* choose relatives as trusted friends. *Trusted friendship requires more than association by birth.* It requires a conscious effort based on mutual needs and trusts.

Occasionally, trusted friendship between relatives may be difficult because of petty jealousies carried on from childhood. If rectification is impossible or has failed, move on to find those who are more sympathetic.

SOME POINTS TO REMEMBER FOR SUCCESSFUL RELATIONSHIPS

1) Be as specific as possible in your request.

2) Ask for what you want. Do not expect others to read your mind.

3. People are different.

4) Respect another's person and property.

5) Show gratitude openly.

6) Avoid boastfulness and arrogance.

7) Avoid whining and complaining.

8) Show affection.

9) Be aware of your moods.

10) Be sensitive to others needs.

11) Keep commitments.

12) Listen.

13) Share your joys as well as your sorrow.

14) Do not take advantage of another's weakness.

15) Admit error openly and freely.

16) Speak in the first person as much as possible.

EGO CONTROL

Successful living requires control of the unruly ego. It is important to develop the capability to give up the ego when necessary, to control it when essential and to enjoy it's benefits. Successful living is hindered by the dominance of ego. Preoccupation with false pride prevents a person from perceiving his *true identity* and cost him dearly in the area of friends.

The Guardians advocate that the ego be controlled. Containment of the ego allows us to operate with power and vitality without arrogance and false pride. When a person is ego-centered there is little room for the *voice* of the Christ Mind.

Look at the ego as your own sense of personal power, compare it to His *almighty power*, then ask yourself which would you choose to be the center of your life.

> **For the heart of this people has become hardened, and they hear with difficulty, and their eyes are dull; so that they cannot see with their eyes and hear with their ears and understand with their hearts; let them return and I will heal them.**
> **—Matthew 13:15**

INSTINCT CONTROL

Within the confines of man's *purpose*, passions and instincts are necessary. When properly satisfied, the energies of the instincts are converted to serve the *divine purpose*, and aid the development of the Christ Mind. As with the ego, the instincts are to be guided by the Christ Mind.

The Guardians suggest that one should be wary of *foolish passion*. *Foolish passion* utilizes excessive energy and does not provide real satisfaction. To gain complete cooperation of the instincts, it is necessary to respect their dignity by fulfilling their desires under His *will*. The vital light is brightened by the willful and prudent satisfaction of the instincts.

MIND CONTROL

In addition to guiding the ego and instincts, it is necessary to contain and control the *mental processes*. The mental faculty is often full of incorrect information learned by blind imitation, rote memorization, false assumptions, and preconceptions. While the mind's capability is great, it's contents and mode of operation can interfere with successful living.

The mind is very useful for its intended purpose, but it must not get into the habit of operating independently from the Christ Mind.

It is hard for the person who prides himself on his intellect to find the Christ Mind within unless he develops humility; for the human intellect is insignificant compared to the wisdom and power of the Christ Mind.

LIMITATIONS OF LOGIC AND REASON

Logic and reason have their limitations and a wise man/woman doesn't misuse this mental faculty.

SUCCESSFUL LIVING REQUIRES DETERMINATION

**Nothing in the world
can take the place
of Persistence.**

**Talent will not;
nothing is more common
than unsuccessful men
with talent.**

**Genius will not;
unrewarded genius
is almost a proverb.**

**Education will not;
the world is full
of educated derelicts.**

**Persistence and Determination alone
are Omnipotent.**

—**Calvin Collidge**
30th President of U.S.A.

This poem states the truth simply. No matter how intelligent a person is, it is the spiritual strength of the Christ Mind, coupled with persistence and determination, which will guarantee successful living.

Chapter 3

Theory and Methods of Adoration

If you wish to contact a friend, for most of you the quickest and most effective way is to ring them on the telephone. Should your friend work in a large office with many lines a button will light up on the instrument on his desk, indicating that a call is waiting.

Adoration is similar to ringing your friend on the telephone. It is the quickest and most effective way of making contact with your Christ Mind. Your Christ Mind is always there, always ready to answer your call—but it is you who must initiate the contact if your wish to receive all the benefits that are available to you by consciously forging a link with this *magnificent power*.

It helps to visualize the Christ Mind. To visualize means to form a mental picture. For many of you this may be difficult at first. Don't be discouraged. Simply silently describe the Christ Mind in words. As you do this day after day it will become increasingly easier to actually form a mental image of His *majesty* and *glory*.

You may visualize Him as both within you and/or without you—for He is both. A stream of *light* from your heart is anchored within your heart. He is also above you and around you, for His *presence* is everywhere.

But for the present think of Him as a *magnificent* being awesome in His *majesty* and *beauty*, radiant with *dazzling light*. See Him clothed in sumptuous garments of silk, adorned with jewels and gold. You may, if you wish, change the color of these garments depending on your need, *for colors are forces of energy, and visualizing them helps release their power.*

Should you simply wish to adore—and this is the purest form of *love*, simply giving *love* for the sheer joy of loving—see Him clad in royal purple and gold. Use the same colors if you are lacking in self-esteem. If your need be money, let Him be clad in green and gold—but always so dazzling with *light* that the colors are almost blinding in their radiance.

The more you pour out *love* and *adoration* to the Christ Mind, the more you will receive, for *love* begets *love*. Love keeps the channel open, so the more you give the more you are able to receive.

All your exercises should be preceded by *adoration* to this great *God-presence* within the heart of your *being*, who is responsible for your very existence.

A number of *adorations* are given below. As you become familiar with this method of pouring out your *love* and *gratitude* to the Christ Mind, you will in time form your own *adorations*. Meanwhile you can vary the ones you use from time to time, selecting from those below. In addition to the longer ones there are some mini-adorations included. These should be memorized and used frequently during the day. Learn to give praise and thanks and pour out your *love* all during the day. The more you adore the Christ Mind, the more quickly you can become truly aware of His *power* and *presence* and draw upon them in time of need.

Some short *adorations* are included which you can easily memorize. Train yourself so that your first thought in the morning as you awaken will be an *adoration* of the Christ Mind, as well as the last thought when you slip into sleep at night.

ADORATION

**Oh, thou Great and Glorious one, father of
the creative spark within my soul.
I Adore Thee and I invoke Thee.
Thou who are un-named and nameless
for Eternity, all-wise, all-powerful,
to Thee I send a flame of Love,
from my Heart to Thy Heart
that we may merge and become in Fact
the One that we are in Truth.
With my mind I know that we are One
else I would not exist;
but I ask Thy Grace that I may fully
believe with all my heart
that we ARE One.**

**For it is then that the Fullness of Thy
Mighty Power can fill my Life with Peace,
Harmony, Love and Success,
all of which I shall endeavor to use to the
Glory of Thine ineffable Name.**

ADORATION

Thou who are the Creator of the Universe and
Center of my Being,
I adore Thee and I invoke Thee.
Oh my Beloved, how could I not love Thee
whose love is so great for me.
It is Thee who never forsakes me,
Thee who supplies all my needs,
Thee who comforts me when I am sad,
Whose Wisdom guides me when I am Confused
and insecure.
It is Thee, my Great and Glorious One,
who fights my battles for me.
It is Thee who art indeed my Father, Mother,
Lover and Brother.

I enfold Thee with a Flame of Love from my
Heart and I await in turn the down rushing
torrent of your Love that will keep me ever
mindful that any separation exists only in
awareness of Thee, for Thou and I are now
and always have been truly One.

ADORATION

The stars in their Splendor praise thy Glory
as they swing through the firmament,
Oh Thou Great Being whose Love for me
surpasses my understanding.
It is Thou who gives me Strength when I am weak.
Thou who fills me with Courage when I am afraid.
Thou, my Great and Glorious Christ Mind,
who will fight my battles for me while I
remain at peace.
Truly I am humbled before Thy Awesome Presence,

and I pour out my Love to Thee in gratitude
and adoration,
while striving to realize there IS no
separation between us—that Thou and I are
truly One and Indivisible.

ADORATION

Oh my Beloved,
I thank Thee that at last I have discovered
Thy Almighty Love and Power.
I thrill with exaltation as I realize that
always Thou has been the Source of my Being
who exists within me and I in Thee.

Oh, Mighty and Glorious One,
I am beginning to realize I do not have to
search without for answers,
For deep within the recesses of my own Being
where Thou abidest, can I find the fulfillment
of all my Desires.
I am grateful that the Dazzling Light of Thy Love
is beginning to illuminate me from within.
Only then can I see clearly and Know with
an Inner Knowing that requires no outer
confirmation that Thou and I are One.

I am humbled with Gratitude to think that
with Thy Gracious Help someday I shall be
more than human and fully understand that
meaning of the question: Know ye not that ye
are gods?

A number of brief adorations follow. These you can and should easily memorize and use often. Remember always, the more love you pour forth to the Christ Mind, the more you are able to receive, for He is an endless fount of blessing. It is you who have to open your heart and your being so that you are able to receive the infinite *love* and *power* He has been waiting to pour out to you. But this He could not do until you were ready to awaken to His *presence* within you.

> **Great Dazzling Radiant Glorious One**
> **I give thanks continually**
> **That Thou are mine and I am Thine**
> **Throughout Eternity.**

> **All Wise, All Merciful, and All Powerful One**
> **I love you, I love you, I love you;**
> **I praise you, I praise you, I praise you**
> **I thank you, I thank you, I thank you**
> **For all the blessings I have received**
> **And all that are yet to come.**
> **Beloved Wise and Magnificent One,**
> **If Myself is Thyself**
> **And Thyself is Myself**
> **Then truly we have to be One.**
> **Thy Power is My Power**
> **Thy Glory is My Glory—**
> **And I am Divine—but I knew it not.**

> **All Praise and Glory be to Thee**
> **Benevolent, Wise and Ineffable One**
> **Who guides me and guards me,**

**protects and supplies me
and helps me to love Thee
as Thou lovest Me.**

STOP—BE STILL—AND LISTEN

If you have a good friend you would not keep him long if you insisted on always conducting a monologue with him and never giving him a chance to speak to you in turn.

It is no different with the Christ Mind, the most loving and powerful friend you will ever have, *adoration* and *affirmations* are indeed important. But equally important is your *silence* so that He may speak to you.

One of the most difficult tasks the beginning student has is to **still** the mind so that he can listen to the voice of the Christ Mind. Difficult, yes. But the most rewarding task he can ever set for himself. You have read or heard of the "still small voices within." Perhaps sometimes you have heard it, perhaps you have heeded it; unfortunately many of you have more often ignored it. But this has been the voice of the Christ Mind trying to guide you and comfort you, trying to make you aware of His *presence* within you. Most of mankind is unable to hear it because of the incessant chattering of the mind.

It is difficult to still the mind, difficult to stop the endless chain of thoughts flashing through it at the speed of light—but it is well worth the effort.

One of the first steps in the process of stilling the mind is called *rhythmic breathing*. Sit up straight in a chair or lie down comfortably on a couch or bed and simply breathe in and out while counting one—two—three—four. Inhale to the count of four, then exhale to the count of four. The very act of concentrating on your breathing will help hold the mind steady, and counting while you breathe will make this little discipline even easier.

It is a simple discipline—so simple that its importance is likely to be overlooked. But five minutes morning and night—will go far in helping you to still the mind.

After having practiced this simple technique for a few weeks, **try**—and keep trying, because you are not likely to succeed just at first—to simply **be still** and listen. This is an exercise which will also require persistence. But if you keep at it the rewards will be great. It is in the silence that you will learn the Christ Mind. It is in the silence that you will receive the love that you crave and begin to realize for yourself with an inner knowing that requires no external confirmation, that your Christ Mind **does** exist; that He is indeed a father, mother, lover, and brother. It is here in the silence you will learn for yourself that with His love and power to help you, in truth you need no other.

These are no idle theories. These are principles that work as certainly as you apply them. Principles that work as certainly as the one that enables you to turn on a light switch and illumine a room. But remember—before applying this principle certain conditions have to be met. The power has to be turned on by the utility company, and a light bulb has to be screwed into the lamp. Then and only then will the light come on. On the other hand—all these conditions could be present and if you did not flip on the switch the room would remain in darkness.

So it is with your Christ Mind. If you meet the conditions of love, adoration, affirmation—and silence, you will become aware of His awesome presence within you, and be able to utilize His tremendous power. And your inner being will be filled with light. But if you neglect to fulfill the conditions you can no more make contact with Him than you can illuminate a room if you fail to turn on the light switch.

The choice is yours. Perform these simple exercises that we give you and fill your being with *light* and *power*—a much better way of living than to neglect them and have to continue to struggle along in darkness. Would you not rather live in the *power* of *light*?

Appendix I

The Goals of
The Church of the Guardians*

1. Union with God through the awakening and utilization of the Christ Mind.

We believe that man is joined by the Christ Mind to the Lord. Unity is basic to successful and purposeful living. *Awareness* and *love* of the Christ Mind provide man with the *power* to live victoriously.

2. Deeds and actions in the world.

Man's deeds and actions in this world satisfy God's requirement of love, creation, and obedience. This is expressed by the following:

The Guardians hold that man's duty is to seek and manage God's abundance. (We often refer to this as God's Trust). Man will be judged by God in accordance with how he manages this Trust. The Guardians also be-

---

* A Chartered Church of the United States Ecclesiastical Society and Seminary, Incorporated California.

lieve that our response to human needs and conditions should remain flexible. We constantly re-evaluate the areas of need which may require our assistance.

SOME PRINCIPLES AND BELIEFS OF THE CHURCH OF THE GUARDIANS

a) There is but one Lord to worship and love.

b) Christ is the Son of our Lord and sits at His right side. He resides in men/women as the Christ Mind.

c) Seek his Son for guidance, power, and love. He is the Lord's great gift to man. He is the Christ Mind in all men/women.

d) Immortality is the true promise of our Lord as revealed through his Son.

e) All sins of men are forgivable through acts of deeds, penance, meditation, and prayer.

f) The ways of coming to God through the Christ Mind are:

1. Adoration
2. Affirmation
3. Belief
4. Concentration
5. Determination
6. Meditation
7. Prayer
8. Questioning
9. Removal of Negativism
10. Will
11. Work

Appendix I - The Goals of the Church of the Guardians

g) Rejoice in God's *love*.

h) All truly religious men shall live as one under the canopy of the Lord and his Son.

i) The Christ Mind is within everyone but requires awakening to reap its power.

j) The Lord has provided everything for successful living.

k) A major foundation of the Guardians is found in Genesis 1:28-30. God blessed them and said to them, "Be fruitful and increase, fill the earth and subdue it, rule over the fish in the sea, the birds of heaven, and every living thing that moves upon the earth." God also said, "I give you all plants that bear seed everywhere on the earth, and every tree bearing fruit which yield seed; they shall be yours for food. All green plants I give for food to the wild animals, to all the birds of heaven, and to all reptiles on earth, every living creature."

l) We are required to follow the Lord's Laws and enjoy his abundance.

m) Persistence and determination are valued highly; but, arrogance and complaining should be avoided.

n) Man must learn to treat himself kindly so that he may learn to treat others kindly.

o) Each person should have a project dedicated to the Lord.

Appendix II

Services Available

from The Church of the Guardians and
The United States Ecclesiastical Society and Seminary

1. Prayer Community: This is directed towards the awareness and development of the Christ Mind through scheduled worship. The Seminary has available a series of publications aimed toward the development of the Christ Mind. In addition, we offer a selected reading list which is helpful in this pursuit.

2. Guidance: Individual and group guidance is available to those who seek to improve their lives and join the Christ Mind.

3. Holistic Health: Counseling, Treatment, and Referral Service.

4. Seminary Study: We offer on or off campus supervised study leading towards Ordination and academic accomplishment. Presently, we offer the following degrees: Blended A.A., B.A., D.D., Th.D. Ph.D., Programs in Religious Studies.

Advisors are available to evaluate past course work and experience, previous credits and degrees, equivalency examinations, and any other pertinent information all aimed towards aiding each prospective student in the selection and direction of his particular course of study. To get more information email info@usess.org or through the website: unitedstatesecclesiasticalsocietyandseminary.org

5. Community Action: We engage in the development of projects and other forms of community involvement which are deemed necessary and useful for the community and society at large.

Appendix III

The United States Ecclesiastical Society and Seminary

The Philosophy
of The Church of the Guardians

We as Guardians symbolize the Lord's *trust* in man. As stated in Genesis, the earth with all of it's abundance and containing all His creations has been placed in our hands. This great gift of God is an obligation and a **trust**, much like a legal trust except the creator of the *trust* is our Lord and we are the beneficiaries of the *trust*.

The benefits of the *trust* shall come to us based on how we guard and utilize his abundance in our own personal lives as well as in the lives of others. Hence the term Guardians: We are all assigned to protect and care for the *creation*.

For those who serve and protect the *trust*, under His ancient *law*, the promise of immortality is given. For those who violate the *trust* through disobedience of His *law*, the result is sin and mortality.

The philosophy of the Guardians is simple and all it requires is that His work be done under His *law*. The joy of His abundance both now and in the future shall be yours.

In the very beginning the earth has been man's dominion, to use and enjoy within the principles He set forth. Through man's arrogance and disobedience of the *law*, he has consistently brought pain and heartache to himself and others.

Man has both the potential and ability to perform his trust keeping duties. One of man's greatest errors however, is that when he becomes successful in any way that he has defined, he becomes **arrogant**. He takes his success as his alone. He forgets the **Lords's** gifts and abundance and takes his success to his **ego**, becoming full of pride, not as a *loved one* of the **Lord**, but as creator himself.

Often he greedily continues on this path robbing others of God's abundance through lies, deceit and fraud. He violates the **law** of God and tries to lose himself in possessions, promiscuity, drugs and power. These are the dangers which possess a man with arrogance, greed and guilt. He becomes obsessed, compulsive and egotistical, losing all track of God's gifts; the joy of possessions, the beauty of love, and the celebration of drink. He misuses the gifts of the **Lord**.

He continues with this behavior, captured in wide extremes, swinging madly from one obsession to another and nothing will help him. His only hope is that through adversity he will awake and cleanse himself from his/her own self destruction and deceit to pick up the Lord's banner from the depths of his heart.

More often than not he continues in this madness and only by circumstance is he/she forced to submit. When he looses all his/her wealth, or becomes ill, or looses his family, or he sees death staring him in his face, he then complains to the Lord, and blames Him for his misfortunes, all the time forgetting that he never thanked the Lord in time of good fortune. He cries on his knees in despair, for he is not seeking the Lord, he doesn't seek forgiveness, nor does he allow Him to come in. He instead whines and complains. Here is an example of a man who treats success as his own and failure as the Lords.

The Guardians hold firmly that we are the protectors of His land, His works, and His laws. Our judgement shall be based on the way we manage the Lord's *trust*. Hence a man with great wealth has a greater obligation of *trust* than a poor man, for the wealthy man has been given more of the Lord's abundance. The wealthy man doesn't have to worry about bread or shelter, but he must be on guard that his wealth is viewed as His *trust* to be used under God's *law* to perform good works and to follow His *will*. If he squanders the *trust* he has violated His *law*. If he hordes it he has taken possession of something which doesn't belong to him, it belongs to the Lord. Therefore the wealthy man must be prudent and carefully use his judgement in guarding and using his part of the *trust*. He must aid those around him, help those who are doing the Lord's work, while at the same time enjoying the abundance that has been placed in his hands.

The poor man likewise has his *trust* to manage, in that his *trust* or talents are gifts of God. He has to guard and properly utilize whatever is in his hands. If he is poor he must help with what he has, for often a kind word or deed is worth it's weight in gold.

Whether poor or rich, we must never forget that what we have is a *divine trust* placed in our hands. It is our *test*. We are tested, but we shall never test the Lord. We are the *trustee* of His creations and abundance as well as the physical and spiritual beneficiary of His *love*. Man has forgotten the Lord's *gifts*; he often gives thanks only to himself, infrequently remembering that his Creator has made everything that has been discovered and "Created".

Man was created by the uplifting spirit of the Lord. No other way is possible, for apes will always remain apes until the Lord decides different. When man truly discovers the *genetic code* and learns how to use it, this in no way will make man the Creator; for the code is the Lord's, a gift for man to use under law.

The danger with man's unlocking of the genetic code is man's arrogance. His arrogance will one day scare him to death and then he shall complain and beg with a dead heart and a greedy mind. He has forgotten that he/she was created by the Lord, and was administered to by the Lord and his counsel until he/she was able to care for himself.

Unless otherwise stated, all are His gifts, from man's intellect to spaceships. The *laws* of "nature" are His, not ours, we merely became aware of them after thousands of years work and effort.

The Lord through his mercy and compassion for his creation has uplifted man so that he may tend the Lord's *garden* and do his work. He gave man freewill so that he could better do His work. He did not want a caretaker who was blind, and without freewill. We are his servants, to care and to love Him and his creation. The world is there for man's *dominion*. The use that man makes of this *divine trust* shall surely tell on his soul, for nothing can be hidden from the Lord. Our minds are open books for him to read.

Appendix III - The Philosophy, Precepts and the Essence

As the Church of the Guardians, we have taken the joy of his *trust* seriously, always trying to do his deeds, whether with gold or with heart and hands. Our love of our duty can best be summed up as:

We are the Guardians of the earth,
The protectors of His laws,
Portrayer of His deeds,
Followers of His will,
Doer's in His unchanging love

The United States Ecclesiastical Society and Seminary

The Precepts
of The Church of the Guardians

1. There is but one Lord to worship and love.
2. Nothing is greater than the Lord.
3. The Lord is all powerful.
4. The Lord is with us.
5. His law is higher than any other law.
6. The Lord has counsel.
7. Christ is the son of our Lord, and sits at his right side.
8. Worship no one but the Lord, as the Lord.
   Seek His Son for guidance, aid and love.
   For He is one of the Lord's great gifts to man.
9. Immortality is the true promise of our Lord
   as manifested through his Son.
10. Matter through Spirit is a gift from God.
11. God can make His Spirit known through matter.
12. The Lord chooses prophets.
13. The Lord has His own plan, ways and time table.

14. He is always there but you must let him into your awareness.
15. The greatest allegiance is to the Lord.
16. His enlightenment awaits you, cease fighting and let his essence fill your consciousness.
17. There is no ideal higher than doing the Lord's work.
18. To worship God is to love his creations.
19. Come to God out of love.
20. The Lord has created man and the world. Man holds the world in *trust* for the Lord, during which time man is to enjoy the Lord's abundance and do his deeds under the *law* of God. He will return and reign over the world, which He left in man's *trust*. What man does with this *trust* determines how men shall be judged. The rule then is seek His abundance and do his deeds under His *will* and *law*.
21. The Lord has provided us with everything in His love and abundance.
22. The Lord wants us to follow his *laws* and enjoy His abundance.
23. The Lord requires that we have complete faith.
24. The Lord requires that the purity of our love be shown in our deeds as well as in our hearts. Action speaks louder than words.
25. The Lord receives and rewards those who seek Him completely.
26. Remember the Lord in all you do.
27. Moderation in all things except Him.

Appendix III - The Philosophy, Precepts and the Essence

28. We please Him with work, prayer, and gifts. Meditate and contemplate Him, enjoying his abundance.
29. Persistence and determination are looked upon highly, arrogance and complaining are not.
30. Prepare yourself in this life.
31. Seek the joy of his love and abundance.
32. Live as fully and completely under his law — power with his purpose.
33. Honor the obedient and honorable, be they parent or stranger, however, no one is immune from God's laws.
34. A chosen person is one who chooses God and His Son, follows his laws, and lives in his abundance doing fine deeds.
35. Sacred meditation by repeating his name and visualizing His image purifies man's mind and opens his heart.
36. All sins are forgivable, through deeds, penance, meditation and prayer.
37. Rote prayers, meditations and the like are unacceptable.
38. Petty bickering over religious fact and methodology is foolish and interferes with man doing the Lord's work.
39. Meet the Lord's test with courage, humbleness, and fortitude.
40. Do not misuse His words for your own purposes.
41. Promiscuity is a compulsion which like all compulsions keeps man away from the Lord.
42. Sex under law is discriminating and personal — love under law.

43. The acts of purification—Coming to God:
    A. Faith
    B. Work
    C. Deeds
    D. Joy of His abundance
    E. Prayer
    F. Mission
    G. Meditation—Purification through the use of imagination.
    H. Seeking
    I. Fasting often
    J. Purification through will
    K. Learning through will
44. The old and new Testament are one book and the Lord's message to men.
45. Follow the Ten Commandments and God's laws in their complete context. They are whole and complete.
46. The Bible is non-temporal in essence while certain parts which pertain to i.e., foods that spoil, etc., are temporal in nature in that spoilage is now controllable. This is an example of temporality.
47. God gave man many powers and talents, of which he uses few. Use God's gifts for His *purpose*.
    Life under law.
48. All truly religious men shall live as one, under the canopy of the Lord and his Son.
49. Man shall not test God nor attempt to make bribes with promises or deeds.

Appendix III - The Philosophy, Precepts and the Essence

50. Man can establish a personal covenant with the Lord. However, this must be differentiated from bribery and false promise.
51. True faith in God is demonstrated in the hearts and deeds of man.
52. All men are God's children.
53. Man is not inherently evil, man is capable of doing evil as well as doing good. Man is inherently God's creation.
54. Man has free-will within God's design.
55. Man must learn to treat himself kindly so that he may learn to treat others kindly.
56. We are all important to God, no one goes unloved.
57. Man must do in the world as well as in the heart. Each person shall have a project for the Lord.
58. Except by divine intervention, man learns at his own speed. Revelation is instantaneous complete knowledge.
59. The Church may issue Ecclesiastical Charters.
60. The Church may have specific orders which perform specific tasks.
61. Churches chartered by the Mother Church are partially autonomous from the Mother Church. They must maintain the principles of the church, but are free to choose ceremonies, rituals and specific deeds.
62. The Mother Church is the final authority on all internal disputes.
63. The Church may have Bishops.
64. The Church may contribute to all causes which serve the law.

65. The members of the Church shall give 10% of their earnings to the Church so the Lord's work may be done.
66. The Church shall provide services for it's parishioners.
67. The Church may establish trusts for those who wish to live a cloistered life.
68. Baptism is for believers and is an initiation experience in the Church.
69. Ministers may take vows of poverty.
70. All ministers must be approved by the Mother Church.
71. The Church may have a seminary and train those for the calling. The Church may charge for this training.
72. Ministers ordained by this Church are not required to obtain an ecclesiastical charter from this organization but they must pay their ministerial dues.
73. Ministers must take an oath in the name of the Lord.
74. Women may be ordained.
75. No discrimination of race, creed or religion.
76. We seek the joy and love of learning.
77. We seek the joy of visible fellowship.
78. We seek the joy of private meditation.
79. A major tenet of the Guardians shall be Genesis 1:28-30. God blessed them and said to them *"be fruitful and increase, fill the earth and subdue it, rule over the fist in the sea, the birds of heaven, and every living thing that moves upon the earth"*. God also said, *"I give you all plants that bear seed everywhere on the earth, and every tree bearing fruit which yield seed; they shall be yours for food. All green plants I give for food to the wild animals, to all the birds of heaven, and to all reptiles on earth, every living creature"*.

Appendix III - The Philosophy, Precepts and the Essence 59

80. The Church holds that total, unequivocal freedom to worship and serve the Lord without compulsion or interference from or by the State.
81. All forms of true healing are acceptable.
82. The Lord is love and love is for everyone, including people who are homosexual.
83. Birth control is acceptable and sometimes essential.
84. Abortion is acceptable when necessary to protect the mind and body of the mother.
85. Divorce is acceptable under proper circumstances, i.e., unfaithfulness, incompatibility.
86. Each man shall seek physical and mental health within the confines of moderation. For the spirit resides in the body.
87. Drinking, smoking, etc., is not sinful. Alcoholism, workaholism, misery, spendthriftyness, promiscuity, compulsive gambling, etc., are illnesses. Their result is evil in that they keep men from having consciousness of the Lord.

The United States Ecclesiastical Society and Seminary

The Essence
of The Church of the Guardians

The two principles of the Guardians are:

a) The attainment of *spiritual union* with the Lord and His Christ.

b) Daily activity *guarding* and *administering* His *trust* by *deed* and *action*.

All things follow from here:

Man through his *deeds* and *actions* in this world is doing His *will*. Man is also not of this world, but joined with Christ to the Lord in and by His *divine grace*. The Guardians respond to the *present* needs of the world, therefore our pursuit, deeds and actions vary with the times. Thus the whole of life is the balance between these two principles.

The method of the Guardians in reaching the first principle is through *meditation, prayer, study*, and by assimilating those who have deeper understanding. However, in and of themselves these are not sufficient.

The second principle of deeds and actions requires complete participation in the world, not renunciation of it.

By participation we mean the enjoyment and administration of the *abundance* of the Lord. The Guardian must be involved with the pleasures and struggles of all life, freeing himself from self-worship and childish stubbornness and greed. Also he must involve himself in *loving, teaching, healing*, and *aiding* those who call upon him. Together, they yield to the Guardian the *purpose* and the *power* to accomplish the Lord's *will*.

TO BE IN THE WORLD
BUT NOT OF IT.

Appendix IV

The Academic Programs

The United States Ecclesiastical Society and Seminary is pleased to offer training for the Ministry and Counseling leading to ordination, academic accomplishment and ecclesiastical charter.

Our Goal

The profession of the Ministry, while concerning itself with the teachings and administration of the ordinances and laws of God, is so expansive and encompassing that volumes could be written on the profession itself. We view the ministry as a helping profession guided by the ever changing needs of man and the Laws of God. Therefore, it is very important to us that all perspective students desiring to help others through counseling, guidance, example, sermon

Most USESS programs have open enrollment.

USESS CENTER • 950 South Central Ave., Compton, CA 90220
Tel: (323) 536-7903   Email: info@usess.org
unitedstatesecclesiasticalsocietyandseminary.org

and deed be well trained for his calling. In order to accomplish this in the most effective and meaningful fashion the minister should be well versed in philosophy, psychology, comparative religion, history as well as the Old and New Testaments, and rites and ceremonies of the Minister. This is the philosophy of the Seminary and towards this end we strive to produce graduates that are committed to compassion, forgiveness and transformation.

The United States Ecclesiastical Society and Seminary is a non-denominational, non-profit religious organization. The word "Society" stands for our desire to be unified as Ministers, while still maintaining our uniqueness. The word "Seminary" stands for the place where teaching and training for the Ministry takes place. Prior to the words "Society" and "Seminary" is the word "Ecclesiastical" which to us means the body of our Lord, or church. The church name for the Society is Church of the Guardians.

In our endeavor to provide a complete service to the prospective minister or the person who desires the calling, the Student, Minister or Healing Practitioner i.e., physicians, psychologists, professional counselors, holistic healer, social workers, nurses, chiropractors, para-professionals or lay healers, we offer church charters to those who have met the qualifications of ordination.

Our hope is to guide those who seek the profession of the Ministry or Guardianship through the process of ordination and academic accomplishment and the subsequent establishment of a branch or chartered church of the United States Ecclesiastical Society and Seminary.

In addition to our Seminary work we have through our founding organization, the Church of the Guardians, been involved with many worthy goals, such as national health, orphan support, rehabilitation, counseling, medicine, scholarships, drug awareness, support of cancer research and awards to outstanding citizens.

To our joy we can now offer to many people who have wished for a career in the Ministry, the opportunity to realize their ambition. Our hope is to make available to you a reputable organization for obtaining your ordination, church charter, and academic enrichment without being restricted by financial conditions, work obligations or the difficulties associated with attending on campus or in-house programs.

Presently we offer the following:
- a. Ordination
- b. Associate Degree of Religious Studies and Ordination
- c. Bachelor Degree of Religious Studies and Ordination
- d. Doctor of Theology and Ordination
- e. Doctor of Philosophy and Ordination
- f. Doctor of Divinity and Ordination
- g. Ecclesiastical Charter

These are all earned degrees which require both course work and practical experience.

Accreditation Information

The United States Ecclesiastical Society and Seminary is incorporated in the State of California. Under our charter the Seminary is exempt from the Approval of the State Board of Education. While accreditation is not required for a religious institution offering training in the Ministry, the Seminary is actively seeking accreditation, since some students would like to work in a secular setting.

Philosophy of Education
Seminary With and Without Walls

With Walls

We have limited space for students who wish to study at the Seminary. In some cases live in space is available for those who wish to be cloistered while they pursue their goals.

Without Walls

The concept of a Seminary without walls is similar to Universities without walls. The original concept was developed when the academic world realized that real life experience could be equated with credits earned in conventional academic institutions. We at the Seminary are pleased that more and more institutions are realizing that real life experience is of significant value and often outweighs the information and knowledge gathered in traditional course work, therefore most students can achieve their goal in an off campus setting.

Introduction to Curriculum

The curriculum at the seminary has been designed for those students who wish to dedicate their lives in doing the Lord's work. All course work is designed for the student who doesn't have the time or the funds to attend conventional in-house or on-campus programs, yet desires to learn and earn his credentials. Some of the course work can be substituted by documented outside experience, prior education or proficiency examinations. However, we require the same quality of work as if you were attending an in-house or on-campus program. Each student is expected to do his best, since his work will reflect on him as well as our institution.

Process of Registration

Students wishing to enroll in the Seminary shall:
a. Complete the application for enrollment and send it along with copies of any previous degrees
b. Have all transcripts sent to the Seminary
c. Send a $50 non-refundable registration fee
d. Send two recent passport size photographs of yourself (jpegs of photos, 300 dpi)

After all materials are received, an advisor shall review his transcripts, evaluate any equivalency exams and life experiences and the student will be notified within four weeks of his acceptance. He will at this time be notified of the courses he must complete at the Seminary. It is very important to include all experiences which relate to helping people and serving the Lord. Remember, experiences can be translated into credit units. Include length of time (preferably in hours), type of activities, etc. Please include references.

Tuition

All fees are due within 30 days of acceptance to the Seminary. Those who pay the entire tuition within 30 days of acceptance are granted a ten percent discount. For those who are unable to pay the entire amount upon acceptance, a deposit of twenty percent followed by equal monthly payments shall be acceptable. In addition, Seminary finances permitting, small scholarships, fellowships and assistantships will be made available. For those students who pay in advance and later decide to discontinue the program, a prorated refund shall be given for the time remaining of their residency requirements. Live in fees are $600. per month, this includes a room, use of kitchen, library and Seminary space.

Graduation

When the student has satisfactorily completed all course work for his desired objective, he shall be notified of the date of graduation by mail. While we prefer the student to come to the Seminary for a personal graduation, if he is unable due to illness, work, or financial hardship, the degree shall be mailed to him. Graduation and degree fee is $50.

Ecclesiastical Charters

These shall be granted to qualified individuals who are ordained by the United States Ecclesiastical Society and Seminary or has an equivalent ordination. A charter allows you to establish a branch of our church in your community. You may either use our name or you may name your own church as long as the name fits with our principles and it is stated that you are a Branch Order *(see enclosure)*. Once you have received the charter you must keep records of all donation or income. The United States Ecclesiastical Society and Seminary requires a ten percent tithing of all branch churches for it's Mission and Seminary.

Ordination Documents and Renewals

Upon ordination the minister will receive his/her ordination certificate and is required to sign an oath to the Lord. In addition he shall receive an Ecclesiastical Identification Booklet. The Ecclesiastical Identification Booklet is updated yearly by an Ecclesiastical stamp. The fee for the renewal stamp is $50 yearly.

Newsletter and Alumni Society

All students who are ordained, have United States Ecclesiastical Society and Seminary Charters or have earned degrees from the Seminary shall automatically become members of the Ecclesiastical Society Alumni Association and shall receive newsletters detailing our activities.

Definitions

Life Experience: *Related documentable life experiences may be substituted for any course which is followed by an asterisk.*

Related Life Experience: May include but is not limited to; medical, psychological, nursing, ministerial, missionary, counseling, volunteer work, social work, participant/observer, half-way house, rehabilitation, legal, etc.

Previous Course Work: This includes work done at any school, home study courses, junior college, university, or vocational course work. All transcriptions must be sent to this institution for approval.

Equivalency Exams: Any exam for credit offered by any university, corporate or government agency (CLEP) which may meet a requirement shall be accepted for any course followed by an asterisk. In addition we will offer exams to students who feel that their knowledge is sufficient in a particular area.

Types of Students:
  Off Campus - Supervised Study
  On Campus
  Blended Study - *Combination of off Campus and on Campus Study*
  Live-in

Residence Time: This refers to the minimum amount of time a student must be registered with the Seminary.

Expulsion: Any student found guilty of falsifying documents or life experiences shall immediately be expelled without refund of tuition.

Tuition Refund Policys: Refunds are available only to students who withdraw from USESS in accordance with the procedures specified in the College Catalog. The amount of refund will be based on the date on which the "Withdrawal Form" is completed and will be computed according to the following schedule. Be advised it may take up to 30 days to issue a refund after a request has been received and approved.

Refund of Tuition
During the 1st week of class............................ 90%
During the 2nd week of class.......................... 80%
During the 3rd week of class.......................... 70%
During the 4th week of class.......................... 60%
During the 5th week of class.......................... 50%
No refund will be issued after the 5th week

Courses Offered

GENERAL EDUCATION

Students follow a general education curriculum that is grouped into four foundational areas: Humanities, Natural Science, Mathematics, and Political & Social Sciences. Courses offered may vary. Courses that fulfill the General Education requirements are below.

Humanities
COM 102: Public Speaking
COM 303: Introduction to Communication
ENG 101: English Composition
ENG 202: Introduction to Literature
ENG 303: Critical Thinking and Argument

Mathematics
MATH 101: College Math I
MATH 130: Introductory Algebra
MATH 150: Intermediate Algebra
MATH 200: College Algebra
MATH 301: Statistics

Natural Sciences
ANA 105: Anatomy
BIO 101: General Biology
CHEM 101: General Chemistry
PH 300: Physics
PHY 105: Human Physiology

Social & Political Sciences
HIS 202: US History: Past to 1877
HIS 203: US History 1865 - Present
POLS 101: Political Science
PSY 101: Introduction to Psychology
SOC 101: Introduction to Sociology

In the humanities area, students will be exposed to the great philosophical, religious, and literary traditions of the world's civilizations. While all courses will emphasize the importance of the rational aspects of human beings and their mental processes, it is hoped that students will also—by studying the fine arts and other subjects in the humanities—develop an appreciation for the great expressions of the human spirit.

The social and political sciences are designed to help students acquire the knowledge and understanding of their own behavior as individuals and as part of their society, ethnic group, heritage, and world. The study of history of the United States and that of other parts of the world will provide students with knowledge of events, factual information, and further practice in critical thinking and analysis.

The natural sciences and mathematics should enable students to learn to solve problems, acquire analytical skills, gain knowledge of the physical, and develop a true spirit of inquiry. These qualities, we believe, will—along with the other liberal arts—strengthen life-long habits of learning and the continued acquisition of knowledge about the world and themselves.

Humanities

COM 102 Public Speaking　　　3 Credit Units
This course introduces all aspects of effective public speaking including verbal and non-verbal considerations such as tone, diction, command and connection with the audience. Students practice delivering various types of messages in front of groups.
Required textbook: Public Speaking (ISBN: 978-0-07803682-8)

COM 303 Introduction to Communication 3 Credit Units
This course equips students with interpersonal and basic public speaking skills geared to prepare them for work-related interactions involving communication-based, problem-solving skills.
Required textbook: Comm (ISBN: 978-1-28544558-8)

ENG 101 English Composition　　　3 Credit Units
This course incorporates a range of grammar lessons and writing prompts to develop students' ability to create thesis statements, draft and develop paragraphs, and write and revise their own essays.
Required textbook: The Longman Reader and Pearson Writer Bundle (ISBN: 978-111827212)

ENG 202 Introduction to Literature　　3 Credit Units
This course guides the student through reading, understanding, and applying critical theory to the four different types of literature: Fiction, nonfiction,

poetry and drama. Students learn how to apply reading skills. They examine linguistic and structural elements of each type of writing. Various types of fiction are examined as well as types of poetry, theater (drama), and nonfiction. Plot and characterization are discussed. Students discover how to write about literature and demonstrate the ability to write a research paper.
Required textbook: Introduction to Literature (ISBN: 978-1-11182721-2)

ENG 303 Critical Thinking and Argument 3 Credit Units
This course provides the student an opportunity to apply argument theory, critical thinking, and writing skills to a variety of current issues. The student will have the opportunity to not only become familiar with what other writers think about issues, but also have the opportunity to use the critical thinking theories to engage the world around them by exploring, analyzing, and synthesizing their own perspectives.
Required textbook: Think Critically (ISBN: 978-0-205-49098-1)

Mathematics

MATH 101 College Math I 3 Credit Units
This course incorporates basic mathematic principles, theories and computation to develop students' ability to solve algebraic and geometric math problems.
Required textbook: Basic College Mathematics (ISBN: 978-0-321-93190-0)

MATH 130 Introduction to Algebra   3 Credit Units

This course establishes a foundation in algebra and problem solving. Topics include signed numbers, exponents, order of operations, simplifying expressions, solving linear equations and inequations, graphing, formulas, polynomials, and factoring.
Required textbook: Introductory Algebra (ISBN: 978-0-321-59921-6)

MATH 150 Intermediate Algebra   3 Credit Units

The algebra of linear and quadratic equations, graphing, functions, inequalities, rational expressions, radicals, and system of equations. The course emphasizes critical thinking and problem-solving skills.
Required textbook: Intermediate Algebra (ISBN: 978-0-321-61336-3)

MATH 200 College Algebra   3 Credit Units

This course is a continuation of the fundamental concepts of Algebra taught in MATH 130. It covers algebra of matrices, conic sections and systems of nonlinear equations, arithmetic and geometric sequences, mathematical induction, counting techniques, probability and the binomial theorem.

MATH 301 Statistics   3 Credit Units

Prerequisites: Math 150 or its equivalent.
This course is designed to offer students the skills necessary to interpret and critically evaluate statistics commonly used to describe, predict, and evaluate data in an information-driven environment. The focus is on

the conceptual understanding of how statistics can be used and how to evaluate statistical data.
Required textbook: Elementary Statistics: Picturing the World (ISBN: 978-0-321-91121-6)

Natural Sciences

ANA 105: Anatomy　　　　　　3 Credit Units
The topics of this course will include understanding the structures and functions of the skeletal system, muscular system, nervous system, integumentary system, respiratory system, tissues, membranes, and blood. In addition, this course will also include understanding proper use of anatomical terminology.
Required textbook: Human Anatomy (ISBN: 978-0-321-902856)

BIO 101: General Biology　　　　3 Credit Units
This course offers a basic overview of biology which is simple enough for non-science majors and thorough enough to serve as a foundation for those pursuing scientific or medical degrees.
Required textbook: Biology (ISBN: 978-1-133-365536-5)

CHEM 101: General Chemistry　　3 Credit Units
This course includes the introduction to physical and chemical properties of the elements, chemical reactions, gas laws, chemical nomenclature, structure of atoms, chemical bonding, and solutions.

PH 300: Physics   3 Credit Units

This course teaches Physics topics including a prelude of stars and atoms, the Newtonian Universe, a transition to new physics, and the post Newtonian Universe, and finally exploration within the atom, including fusion and fission. The course concludes with a look toward the future.

PHY 105: Human Physiology   3 Credit Units

The topics of this course will include understanding the structures and functions of the skeletal system, muscular system, nervous system, integumentary system, respiratory system, tissues, membranes, and blood. In addition, this course will also include understanding proper use of anatomical terminology.
Required textbook: Human Anatomy (ISBN: 978-0-321-902856)

Social & Political Sciences

HIS 202: US History: Past to 1877   3 Credit Units

This course delivers a broad survey of American history from New World exploration and settlement through the Civil War.
Required textbook: America Past and Present Vol 1 (ISBN: 978-0-205-90519-5)

HIS 203: US History: 1865 - Present   3 Credit Units

This course delivers a broad survey of American history from Civil War to present.
Required textbook: America Past and Present Vol 2 (ISBN: 978-0-205-90547-8)

POLS 101: Political Science   3 Credit Units

> The student examines the concepts and methodology of Political Science as well as the various fields of the disciple including American politics, comparative politics, international politics and political philosophy and the origins of our political values. Students analyze political ideas, theories, ideologies, systems and policies in order to focus on and investigate political problems on a national and global level as well as define central concepts related to the study of political science.

PSY 101: Introduction to Psychology   3 Credit Units

> This course offers comprehensive yet concise overview of the basic principles of psychology.
>
> *Required textbook: Introduction to Psychology (ISBN: 978-1-11183363-3)*

SOC 101: Introduction to Sociology   3 Credit Units

> This course will help students quickly come to see how sociology applies to many areas of their lives and how it is used in day to day activities.
>
> *Required textbook: Sociology - Intro To Sociology (ISBN: 978-1133588085)*

UPPER DIVISION COURSES

100 **Hypnosis**   3 Credit Units

The course will help you to become a hypnotist and cover the methods of hypnotherapy. It will explain what hypnosis is and what it is not. The class will go over the history of hypnosis and hypnosis vocabulary. It will cover the rules of the mind, the pre-induction interview, and mental attitudes. Several different methods of induction and emerging techniques are covered as well as hypnotic depth testing, methods of deepening, direct suggestion techniques, self-hypnosis, and regression techniques. It includes information on the intake forms, client worksheet, and physician referral form. Learn about sports enhancement therapy, fear removal, universal therapy, medical hypnosis, enhancement of productivity and other benefits.

101 **Beginning Acupuncture**   3 Credit Units

This beginning class covers a brief history of Chinese Acupuncture starting with its origins and academic accomplishments. The modern decline as well as the rejuvenation of acupuncture in China is also discussed; followed by the dissemination of acupuncture to the world. This course also covers the Yin-Yang principle and it's application in traditional Chinese medicine. The five elements and the classification of phenomena as well as their law of movement and their application in traditional Chinese medicine is discussed.

* (Life Experience exchange is possible.)

102   **Academic Foundations**   1 Credit Units

In this course, students will learn to read faster for higher comprehension and retention. Students will learn how to take meaningful study notes about what they read, and display a basic knowledge of standard rhetorical principles and elements of various texts. Students are required to critically analyze and respond to nonfiction texts related to the themes of personal and academic success in college.

This course is required of all students during the first semester of study.

201   **Intermediate Acupuncture**   3 Credit Units

This intermediate class covers the classification, production and functions of Qi. It also covers blood and body fluids and the relationship between Qi and blood and body fluids. The course will also teach the basic concepts of the Meridians and Collaterals. Focus will be on their composition and function as well as their distribution and cyclical flow.

301   **Advanced Acupuncture**   3 Credit Units

In this course, students will learn to read faster This advanced class will teach the student the classification and methods of locating acupuncture points as well as proportional measurements and anatomical landmarks of specific acupuncture points. Special emphasis will be placed on the therapeutic properties of the points. Students will learn how to use hand needles on themselves as part of this class (additional equipment maybe required).

* (Life Experience exchange is possible.)

305 Philosophies of the World   4 Credit Units
The study of philosophy from Plato to James. This is an overview course covering major concepts of these thinkers, as well as the development of philosophical principals. Successful completion of this course shall be measured by a paper describing the similarities and differences between these thinkers, as well as their contribution to the modern world.

310 Counseling of the Family   6 Credit Units
The student shall find a place in the community where he shall make himself available for five hours a week or more to help those who require aid. He shall do this under the supervision of a physician, counselor, psychologist, minister, nurse, rabbi, or a person similarly qualified. During this period he shall read two major books on family counseling. Successful completion of this course shall be demonstrated by documentation and the recommendation of this supervisor. In addition, a paper (12 pages or more) covering the various approaches used or studied during the training is required. A total of 100 hours supervised counseling is required.*

315 The Theory of Family Life   4 Credit Units
Community work, observation and reading are required in this area. Documentation shall consist of a schedule of activities concerning the family, which when possible consists of certified documents showing the time and quality of the work which the student has done.*

* (Life Experience exchange is possible.)

320   **Human Sexuality**   3 Credit Units
This course involves the study of procreation and sexual experience. If outside documentation is required it must be provided by a physician, nurse or qualified person in the field. Additional documentation may be provided by a licensed psychologist, or marriage family counselor, or the equivalent.*

325   **The Bible**   5 Credit Units
This course involves an intensive study of the Bible; both the Old and New Testaments.

350   **Personality Theory I**   4 Credit Units
General overview of the psychological theories which affect the individual in his/her adaptation to life. Successful completion of this course requires a 30 page or larger paper discussing the various theories studied as they relate to daily life.

350   **Personality Theory II**   4 Credit Units
This course is the continuation of Personality Theory I curriculum involving more breadth and depth.

370   **Politics, Sociology and Anthropology** 4 Credit Units
This course consists of general readings of the theories of politics, society, and culture as they effect religion in modern times.

400   **Comparative Religions**   5 Credit Units
This course consists of the study of at least three religions. A paper comparing and contrasting them will be required.

---

* (Life Experience exchange is possible.)

Appendix IV - The Academic Programs

410 **The Old Testament** 4 Credit Units
A complete reading of the Old Testament.*

415 **The New Testament** 4 Credit Units
A complete reading of the New Testament.*

420 **The Koran and Buddhist Bible** 3 Credit Units
A complete reading of the above texts.

425 **Duties and Rituals of the Minister-Priest I**
5 Credit Units
This course shall cover the duties and rituals of the Minister-Priest. The student may practice on tapes or write papers on the use of proper passages covering particular rites. In addition he shall practice healing, marriage, baptismal, and burial service.*

430 **Duties and Rituals of the Minister-Priest II**
5 Credit Units
This course is the continuation of the Duties and Rituals of the Minister-Priest I curriculum involving more breadth and depth.*

450 **Inspirational Experiences I** 3 Credit Units
A paper is required describing the inspirational experiences of the student. This must be personal and can relate with the student's experience with God during crisis or under normal circumstances.*

455 **Inspirational Experiences II** 3 Credit Units
This course is the continuation of the Inspirational Experiences I curriculum involving more breadth and depth.

* (Life Experience exchange is possible.)

499   **Capstone Project**   6 Credit Units

The Capstone Project is a two-semester process in which students pursue independent research on a question or problem of their choice, engage with the scholarly debates in the relevant disciplines, and - with the guidance of a faculty mentor - produce a substantial paper that reflects a deep understanding of the topic.

* (Life Experience exchange is possible.)

GRADUATE COURSES

500   **Thesis**   8 Credit Units
A Thesis of 50 pages or more covering the student's life experiences and a topic of personal interest which integrates the covered course work.

605   **Research in Philosophy**   9 Credit Units
This is a broad in-depth course which covers the development of thought. A paper shall be prepared covering the important philosophical issues such as free will/determination, nature/nurture, mind/body/spirit, material and others as outlined by the directors of this institution. This is a broad course and may take the student as long as six months to prepare the document.

610   **Religion and Theosophy**   7 Credit Units
This course is similar to the Research in Philosophy course except the content shall concern itself with the development of Religion and Theosophy. Practical as well as course work experience is necessary. All practical experience shall be documented. In addition, a 40 page paper is required covering the various aspects of religion and Theosophy.*

620   **The Study of Psychotherapy**   5 Credit Units
This course involves a comprehensive study of all schools of Psychotherapy, focused on certain cognitive, behavioral, and emotional regulation techniques. A substantial amount of time will be spent addressing each of the major schools of thought, acknowledging that each has its own strengths and weaknesses. This course will provide you with an introduction to the theories, styles, and methods of psychotherapy that you would need to know in a clinical situation.

* (Life Experience exchange is possible.)

632　**The Essence of Man**　　5 Credit Units
This is a course calling for creativity. The student is required to write a 25 page original work on the nature of man.

640　**Readings**　　3 Credit Units
Readings of the students' choice from the Suggested Book List *beginning on page 97*.*

650　**Writings**　　4 Credit Units
Writings of the students' choice in reference to the Suggested Book List *beginning on page 97*.*

660　**Politics and Society**　　3 Credit Units
This course covers various political and social systems which effect man's Love and Worship of God.

700　**Research**　　5 Credit Units
The student shall select a relevant topic and do research in this area. This is a pre-dissertation course.*

710　**Research Theory and Design**　　5 Credit Units

720　**Research Project**　　5 Credit Units

725　**Intensive One Week Seminar**　　5 Credit Units

730　**Dissertation**　　15 Credit Units
A comprehensive research project which shall be prefaced by a history of the student's life, including personal joy and struggles. The body of the dissertation must be original and written in such a fashion that it may be published.

Ordination

The definition of Ordination is "the rite of consecration to the Ministry". This means a ceremony which sets apart as sacred, a person who believes in His work and is authorized to teach and administer the ordinances of God. Therefore, ordination by the Society is not taken lightly.

Ordination requirements:

One year of study and 30 semester units or the equivalent (two years of work experience are equivalent to one year of college). Any substitutions acquired by work experience, or other such experience, must be accompanied by appropriate documents. This shall include but is not limited to:

1. A Personal sworn oath
2. Employer's letter of verification
3. Personal references from three people
4. Transcripts of college credits.

Course Work

Course No.	Course Name	Credit Units
102	**Academic Foundations**	1
310	**Counseling of the Family**	6
315	**The Theory of Family Life**	4
320	**Human Sexuality**	3
325	**The Bible**	5
350	**Personality Theory I**	4
425	**Duties and Rituals of the Minister-Priest I**	4
450	**Inspirational Experiences I**	3

Total Credit Units 30

Tuition for Ordination

Tuition is $100 per unit and covers verification and evaluation of prior experiences, advisor guidance, transcript preparation, tutorial, personal consultation and the ordination ceremony. Any required reading material, or traveling expenses, are not covered. If financial problems exist, a payment schedule is available. If you are unable to travel due to illness or financial conditions, ordination may be accomplished by a conference telephone call.

Associate Degree of Religious Studies & Ordination

Requirements: Two years of study or 60 semester units and the following required courses. Some of this requirement may be met by years of documented related work experience.

Course Work

Course No.	Course Name	Credit Units
	12 General Education Classes* *(3 from each area)*	36
102	Academic Foundations	1
310	Counseling of the Family	6
320	Human Sexuality	3
325	The Bible	5
415	The New Testament	3
499	Capstone Project	6

Total Credit Units 60

Tuition for Associate Degree of Religious Studies & Ordination

The tuition for this program is $100 per unit. Residence requirement is one year but this may be more or less depending on the students previous accomplishments and documented related work experience.

*See General Education Classes beginning on page 71.

Bachelors Degree of Religious Studies & Ordination

Requirements: All requirements of the Associate Degree of Religious Studies and the following:

Two years of college or 60 semester units. Some of this requirement may be met by years of documented related work experience.

Course Work

Course No.	Course Name	Credit Units
	4 Electives	12
	4 General Education Classes* *(1 from each area)*	12
305	Philosophies of the World	4
315	The Theory of Family Life	4
350	Personality Theory I	4
410	The Old Testament	4
425	Duties and Rituals of the Minister-Priest I	5
450	Inspirational Experiences I	3
455	Politics, Sociology and Anthropology	4
500	Thesis	8
	Total Credit Units	60

Tuition for Bachelors Degree of Religious Studies and Ordination

The tuition for this program is $200 per unit. Residence requirement is three years but this may be more or less depending on the students previous accomplishments and documented related work experience.

*See General Education Classes beginning on page 6.

Doctorate Degrees

The United States Ecclesiastical Society and Seminary offers three earned Doctorate degrees.

The degrees offered are:
Th.D. Doctor of Theology
Ph.D. Doctor of Philosophy
and D.D. Doctor of Divinity

Doctor of Theology

Requirements:

1. A Bachelor's degree plus the equivalent of 30 credit units or a Master's degree acceptable to this institution, or the equivalent of 150 credit units, and or equivalency exams or related life experiences.

2. Ordination acceptable to this institution. If not ordained the following courses may be required:

Course No.	Course Name	Credit Units
310	Counseling of the Family	6
325	The Bible	5
400	Comparative Religions	5

3. Course work as outlined on next page.

Course Work

Course No.	Course Name	Credit Units
102	Academic Foundations	1
410	The Old Testament	4
415	The New Testament	4
420	The Koran and Buddhist Bible	3
450	Inspirational Experiences I	3
500	Thesis	8
610	Religion and Theosophy	7
632	The Essence of Man	5
710	Research Theory and Design	5
720	Research Project	5
725	Intensive One Week Seminar	5
730	Dissertation	15

Total Credit Units 65

After completion of the above course work, an oral or written exam shall be given and if the student passes he shall be granted the degree of Th.D., Doctor of Theology.

Tuition for Doctor of Theology

The tuition for this program is $200 per unit. Residence time is 24 months but may vary depending on the student's past academic and life experiences. The cost shall include all consultations, tutorial, record keeping, certification of documentations, degree award, exams, and if required a one week intensive seminar. All traveling expenses, phone charges and reading materials shall be paid for by the student.

Doctor of Philosophy

Requirements:

1. A Bachelor's degree plus the equivalent of 30 credit units or a Master's degree acceptable to this institution, or the equivalent of 150 credit units, and or equivalent related experiences or exams.

2. Course work as outlined.

Course Work

Course No.	Course Name	Credit Units
102	**Academic Foundations**	1
605	**Research in Philosophy**	9
610	**Religion and Theosophy**	7
620	**The Study of Psychotherapy**	5
640	**Readings** *(from the Suggested Book List)*	3
650	**Writings** *(in reference to the Suggested Book List)*	4
660	**Politics and Society**	3
700	**Research**	5
710	**Research Theory and Design**	5
720	**Research Project**	5
725	**Intensive One Week Seminar**	5
730	**Dissertation**	15

Total Credit Units 67

After completion of the above course work, an oral or written exam shall be given and if the student passes he shall be granted the degree of Ph.D., Doctor of Philosophy.

Tuition for Doctor of Philosophy

The tuition for this program is $200 per unit. Residence time is 24 months but may vary depending on the student's past academic and life experiences. The cost shall include all consultations, tutorial, record keeping, certification of documentations, degree award, exams, and if required a one week intensive seminar. All phone expenses, traveling expenses and other outside reading materials shall be paid for by the student.

Doctor of Divinity

Requirements:

1. A Bachelor's degree plus the equivalent of 30 credit units or a Master's degree acceptable to this institution, or the equivalent of 150 credit units, and or equivalent related experiences or exams.

2. Ordination acceptable to this institution. If not ordained the following courses may be required:

Course No.	Course Name	Credit Units
310	Counseling of the Family	6
325	The Bible	5
400	Comparative Religions	5

3. Course work as outlined.

Course Work

Course No.	Course Name	Credit Units
102	Academic Foundations	1
410	The Old Testament	4
415	The New Testament	3
420	The Koran and Buddhist Bible	3
425	Duties and Rituals of the Minister-Priest I	5
430	Duties and Rituals of the Minister-Priest II	5
450	Inspirational Experiences I	5
455	Inspirational Experiences II	5
500	Thesis	8
640	Readings *(from the Suggested Book List)*	3
650	Writings *(in reference to the Suggested Book List)*	4
725	Intensive One Week Seminar	5
730	Dissertation	15

Total Credit Units 66

After completion of the above course work, an oral or written exam shall be given and if the student passes he shall be granted the degree of D.D., Doctor of Divinity.

Tuition for Doctor of Divinity

The tuition for this course is $200 per unit. Residence time is 24 months but may vary depending on the student's past academic and life experiences. The cost shall include all consultations, tutorial, record keeping, certification of documentations, degree award, and exams. All traveling expenses and other outside reading materials shall be paid for by the student, if required. Housing and food for a one week seminar shall be paid by the student.

USESS IS NOT ACCREDITED BY AN ACCREDITING AGENCY RECOGNIZED BY THE UNITED STATES SECRETARY OF EDUCATION.

LEGAL STATUS
UNITED STATES ECCLESIASTICAL SOCIETY and SEMINARY is a nonprofit institution, owned, controlled, administrated, maintained and lawfully operating as a nonprofit religious corporation who has submitted information and Declaration for Religious Exemption in the following states;
STATE OF CALIFORNIA
Bureau for Private Post-Secondary and Vocational Education
400 R Street Suite 5000
Sacramento, CA 95814

Selected Book List

Gordon W. Allport
The Nature of Prejudice, 1958

Issac Asimov
Guide to the Bible: The Old Testament, 1969

Revised Standard Bible

John Brown
The Suffering And The Glories of The Messiah, 1981

Martin Buber
I And Thou, 1937

D. A. Carson and Douglas. J. Moo
An Introduction to the New Testament, 2005

Rudolf. Ekstein
The Challenge: Despair and Hope in The Conquest of Inner Space, 1971

Dion Fortune
The Mystical Qabalah, 1976

Erich Fromm
Man For Himself, 1947
The Art of Loving, 1956

J. K. Galbraith
The Affluent Society, 1967

Benjamin Graber M.D., and Georgia Kline-Graber R.N.
Woman's Orgasm, 1975

Dwight Goddard
The Buddhist Bible

Wayne Grudem
Systematic Theology: An Introduction to Biblical Doctrine, 2009

Harold J. Haas
Pastoral Counseling, 1970

George Howie
St. Augustine on Education, 1969

Abraham Jacobson/Christopher Hyatt
A Modern Jew in Search of a Soul, 1986

William James
The Varieties of Religious Experiences, 1902

Masters and Johnson
Human Sexual Response, 1966

Carl Jung
Two Essays on Analytical Psychology, 1966

Bob Kelleman, PhD.
Soul Physicians: A Theology of Soul Care and Spiritual Direction, 2007

Sheldon B. Kopp
If You Meet The Buddha On The Road Kill Him: The Pilgrimage of Psychotherapy Patients, 1972

The Koran

Elisabeth Kübler-Ross
On Death and Dying, 1969

Calvin S. Hall, Gardner Lidzey and John B. Campbell
The Theories of Personality, 1957, 1998

Alexander Maclaren
Maclaren's Sermon Outlines: A Choice Collection of 35 Model Sermons, 1954

Rollo May
The Art of Counseling, 1939

Osho
Rebellion, Revolution and Religiousness, 1990

Francis Regardie
The Romance of Metaphysics: An Introduction to the History, Theory and Psychology of Modern Metaphysics, 1946

Wilhelm Reich
The Murder of Christ, 1953
The Mass Psychology of Fascism, 1933

Carl Rogers
On Becoming A Person, 1961

Lee Rosten
Religions of America, 1975

Richard W. Roukema, M.D.
Counseling For The Soul In Distress—What Every Pastoral Counselor Should Know About Emotional and Mental Illness, 2nd Edition, 2003

Bertrand Russel
The History of Western Philosophy, 1972

Jean-Paul Sarte
Anti-Semite and Jew, 1965

Gershon Scholem
Major Trends in Jewish Mysticism, 1941

F. M. Schweitzer
A History of The Jews, 1971

George Seldes
The Great Quotations, 1960

Sri Daya Mata
Only Love, 1976

Sri Gyanamata
God Alone: The Life and Letters of a Saint, 1984

Paul Tilllich
Courage To Be, 1952

Eckhart Tolle
A New Earth, 2005
Stillness Speaks, 2003

Uccocil
Book of Worship: United Church of Christ, 1986
(Students' Denomination)

Merrill F. Unger
Unger's Bible Handbook, 1966

Charles L. Wallis
The Minister's Manual (Doran's), 1947

John H. Walton and Andrew E. Hill
Old Testament Today, 2006

Max Weber
The Protestant Ethic and The Spirit of Capitalism, 1958

Paramahansa Yogananda
Autobiography of a Yogi, 1946
Where There Is Light, 1988